Moments
of Mindfulness

*Find a Little Stillness
in a Busy World*

Leaping Hare Press

This edition published in the UK and North America in 2016 by

Leaping Hare Press

An imprint of The Quarto Group
The Old Brewery, 6 Blundell Street
London N7 9BH, United Kingdom
T (0)20 7700 6700 **F** (0)20 7700 8066
www.QuartoKnows.com

First published in the UK in 2015

Text copyright © Maria Arpa 2012 & 2013, Peter Bridgewater 2015,
Clea Danaan 2010, Wendy Ann Greenhalgh 2015, Mike Fisher 2012,
Adam Ford 2011 & 2013, Richard Gilpin 2012, The Happy Buddha
2011, Ben Irvine 2012, Satish Kumar 2013, Mark Magill 2010,
Julia Ponsonby 2014, Ark Redwood 2011, Claire Thompson 2013
Design and layout copyright © 2017 Quarto Publishing plc

This book was conceived, designed and produced by

Leaping Hare Press

58 West Street, Brighton BN1 2RA, United Kingdom

Creative Director PETER BRIDGEWATER
Publisher SUSAN KELLY
Editorial Director TOM KITCH
Art Director WAYNE BLADES
Series Commissioning Editor MONICA PERDONI
Designer GINNY ZEAL
Illustrators CLIFFORD HARPER & SARAH YOUNG

British Library Cataloguing-in-Publication Data
A catalogue record for this book is available from
the British Library

ISBN: 978-1-78240-251-0

Printed in China

5 7 9 10 8 6

Contents

FOREWORD

Mindfulness. Defined as the simple act of being conscious, or aware. Perhaps you have already heard of it? It is an ancient spiritual practice, rooted in early Buddhism, that is currently enjoying a great resurgence of interest. Does this make it a passing fad, perhaps? Not if we are wise – because the act of mindfulness is also a very practical skill that people in all walks of life can learn, from the devout to the atheist, the pressured doctor to the harassed parent, the labourer to the academic. Mindfulness is for all those who want to find balance and poise in their lives, to live more consciously, to find some deeper meaning to illuminate the daily toil. And – dare we say it? – to endeavour to discover true happiness.

ॐ A key aspect of mindfulness – and perhaps the feature that makes it so relevant to modern living – is that it is easily integrated into whatever we are doing. Working, gardening, beekeeping, baking, walking, cycling, engaging with the natural world. It can help us to be more conscious of how we handle our relationships, including parenting our children; and it can help us overcome personal challenges such as anger, depression, even bereavement. Inhale, exhale, relax. The past is behind us, the future not yet here – we're in the present moment, the here and now.

ॐ As we practice mindfulness, we become increasingly aware of how flustered we have been, how ill at ease, how full of anxiety and worry; of how we constantly seek to distract ourselves, seemingly unable to let silence settle within us. We switch on the radio or TV, we grab a magazine, we pop out to the shops, we do anything to divert our attention from the one thing that can be deeply healing – stillness. It is in stillness that we discover a deep sense of well-being. And from a point of stillness, we send out ripples that transform our lives for the better.

❧ The message of mindfulness is as important now as it was three and a half thousand years ago, when the Buddha first delivered it to a community experiencing great economic change and the old religions were being questioned; when people were searching for a new spirituality. We, too, are living through a period of great social change, and there is a growing desire to wake up to what is going on in our lives, in our communities, and across the planet — to take responsibility for ourselves and our environment. The aphorisms collected in this book gently affirm that living mindfully helps us achieve that desire.

ADAM FORD Author of *Mindfulness & The Art of Urban Living*, *The Art of Mindful Silence*, *The Art of Mindful Walking* and *Galileo & The Art of Ageing Mindfully*.

INTRODUCTION

What do you like to do with downtime? If you like baking bread, then sorting out and weighing the ingredients, following the recipe, kneading the dough and baking the loaf are all therapeutic. You need to focus and be calm, and at the end of the process you have a finished product that you can share and enjoy. Although you may never have initially thought of it in that way, baking has all the ingredients for a mindful meditation.

❧ How long is it since you did something with the total but relaxed awareness that is a hallmark of mindfulness? If you can't remember, or it seems like a long time ago, you need a reminder of the everyday quality of awareness. It doesn't have to be kept for best, or saved for a moment that's naturally peaceful; it can be found in all sorts of activities or reflections. You can indulge in it in the here and now. In fact, that's the best place for it.

 So what's the best way to invite mindfulness into your daily life? Everyone has their own ideas, and *Moments of Mindfulness* brings together a collection of the best: small, individual insights from a collective of authors on a wide range of topics, from cycling to reflections on the natural world, and from walking to the art of beekeeping. They prove that an alternative way of thinking, feeling and living is possible, and you will find inspiration in all their moments, whether they are reflecting on the joy of freedom on two wheels, taking the time to truly notice a patch of sunlight on a leafy bough, or understanding where less positive thoughts — anger, or depression — come from, and how to let them pass through you without causing damage. This is mindful living of the best kind, offering more than just taking stock and saying 'om'. Taking up these moments will help you to pause, breathe, focus and return to your routine refreshed and energized.

❧ What about the wider world? One of the blocks you may come up against when setting out to enjoy mindfulness in small doses is the idea that we all need to be part of a larger crusade to try and change the world. Somehow, the thinking goes, mindfulness only counts if it's part of a big movement against the hectic pace, the encroaching stress and the perpetual pressure that seem to be unavoidable parts of modern life. But in reality, there's no contradiction: the mantra 'do no harm' holds just as much value in small actions or thoughts as in big ones. Mindfulness breeds mindfulness, and it works as well or better if you start small.

❧ Stillness is the key to well-being. If you learn to use even little fragments of time usefully — to stop, look around you and to feel where you are, to connect with a particular observation or activity — it can have a wonderfully positive effect on your health and happiness. It feels like a gift: you haven't invested a lot of time or strenuous thinking, but the benefits are immediate and palpable. Let *Moments of Mindfulness* be your guide, and learn to make the most of your time, experiencing life to the full, even when you have only ten minutes to spare.

CHAPTER ONE

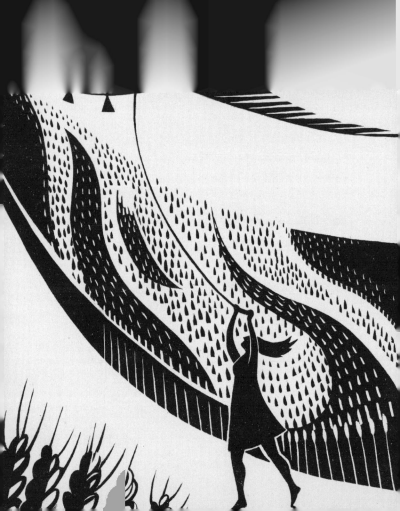

FINDING
CONTENTMENT

BEFORE WE CAN BE HAPPY,
WE NEED TO LEARN HOW WE MAKE
OURSELVES UNHAPPY, AND AS WE SEE
THIS WE STOP DOING IT TO OURSELVES.
IT SOUNDS SIMPLE, AND IT IS, ONCE YOU
RECOGNIZE WHAT HAS BROUGHT
YOU TO YOUR UNNATURAL STATE
OF UNHAPPINESS.

HAPPINESS

Being here and now, with life simply as it is,

is the paradise we have been seeking.

FROM 'HAPPINESS & HOW IT HAPPENS'
THE HAPPY BUDDHA

REFLECTION

*If one is unhappy, one wants to know
the reason why. But it never occurs to one to
ask why one is happy. It is therefore unhappiness,
rather than happiness, that causes us to reflect
upon our condition. It is unhappiness that
makes us think.*

SANGHARAKSHITA

PURE AWARENESS

◆

There is not a fixed identity within,
even though we may very much feel that
there is. We are really a flow of ever-changing
moods, feelings, emotions and thoughts; 'behind'
or 'beyond' thoughts and feelings there is
awareness that remains unaffected by
any number of 'bad' experiences.

FROM 'HAPPINESS & HOW IT HAPPENS'
THE HAPPY BUDDHA

MIND CHATTER

If your mind is busy, then you can simply notice that your mind is busy. Thoughts are not a problem once we begin to leave them alone. When we can simply let them be without taking them all so seriously, they begin to die down of their own accord.

FROM 'HAPPINESS & HOW IT HAPPENS'
THE HAPPY BUDDHA

ACCEPTANCE

---

*If we can accept life, accept ourselves,
this is the end of conflict. Happiness and freedom
are present right now if only we can learn to
accept the 'unacceptable'.*

FROM 'HAPPINESS & HOW IT HAPPENS'
THE HAPPY BUDDHA

Play

---◆---

*Take time out to do the simple things you
love to do — the things that satisfy your heart.
Learn to play.*

FROM 'HAPPINESS & HOW IT HAPPENS'
THE HAPPY BUDDHA

TRUST IN AWARENESS

*We are all addicted to thinking about life.
It takes a lot of trust to stop trying to work
everything out and simply dwell in the present
moment; but behind the usual incessant thinking
is a greater intelligence we can trust.*

FROM 'HAPPINESS & HOW IT HAPPENS'
THE HAPPY BUDDHA

KNOW YOUR FEAR

*Fear keeps us small and prevents us from
living open, happy and fulfilling lives. Fear is
the trigger for many of our actions, and the root
of all violence. If you face your fear, and see it
for what it is, you will become free of it.*

FROM 'HAPPINESS & HOW IT HAPPENS'
THE HAPPY BUDDHA

ENOUGH

◆

*Through the practice of mindfulness and
self-control we cease being slaves to materialism
and our wants, and we learn the meaning
of three very beautiful words —
I Have Enough.*

FROM 'HAPPINESS & HOW IT HAPPENS'
THE HAPPY BUDDHA

HEALING

◆

Welcome everything about yourself: the good,
the bad and the ugly. It is the only way that our
lives truly heal. It is the only way that inner
'enemies' transform into friends and allies
that accompany us in harmony
on our journey.

FROM 'HAPPINESS & HOW IT HAPPENS'
THE HAPPY BUDDHA

WAKE UP & LET GO

*Let go of the bundle of lifelong habits
that cause you suffering and unhappiness.
Let go of all the limiting views that lead
you to live a small, fearful and
cramped life. Let go of the self.*

FROM 'HAPPINESS & HOW IT HAPPENS'
THE HAPPY BUDDHA

INNER SILENCE

◆

Before we can carry our own inner silence
out into the noisy world, we need to identify it,
to know it as a friend. Everyone who has found
this inner silence will have discovered it in their
own different way. We can find it even when
simply standing by a gatepost.

FROM 'SEEKING SILENCE IN A NOISY WORLD'
ADAM FORD

CHAPTER TWO

RESTORING HOPE IN THE FACE OF GRIEF

WE REJOICE AT THE TIME OF BIRTH
BUT THERE CAN BE NO BIRTH WITHOUT
DEATH. WE SHOULD CELEBRATE DEATH
AS THE ACCOMPLISHMENT OF
LIFE'S JOURNEY.

RIDING THE STORM

We must allow ourselves to ride out the storm — not fight or oppress it. Even the darkest storm doesn't last forever.

FROM 'MINDFULNESS & THE JOURNEY OF BEREAVEMENT'
PETER BRIDGEWATER

GRIEVING MINDFULLY

◆

*Grieving mindfully is a process of
gently putting the pieces back together again,
consciously, fully appreciating what we
have lost and giving us insight into
who we are.*

FROM 'MINDFULNESS & THE JOURNEY OF BEREAVEMENT'
PETER BRIDGEWATER

HOPE

As long as there is life, there is hope.

As long as there is hope, there is life.

Hope is our fountainhead.

FROM 'MINDFULNESS & THE JOURNEY OF BEREAVEMENT'
PETER BRIDGEWATER

CONTINUAL FLUX

Death helps us to realize that everything around us is in a state of continual flux and that nothing in life is guaranteed or permanent.

FROM 'MINDFULNESS & THE JOURNEY OF BEREAVEMENT'
PETER BRIDGEWATER

OPENING TO REALITY

We shouldn't fight grief but rather
open ourselves up to reality, however painful.

FROM 'MINDFULNESS & THE JOURNEY OF BEREAVEMENT'
PETER BRIDGEWATER

A JOURNEY

Bereavement is a personal journey,
as individual and unique as each life and
every relationship.

FROM 'MINDFULNESS & THE JOURNEY OF BEREAVEMENT'
PETER BRIDGEWATER

ACCEPTING LOSS

We must accept death as a natural process from which there is no hiding place. Dying is as much a part of life as living.

FROM 'MINDFULNESS & THE JOURNEY OF BEREAVEMENT'
PETER BRIDGEWATER

ALLOWING PAIN

The intense pain of loss is only temporary. We must fully experience our journey of suffering. Mindfulness enables us to walk through our grief.

FROM 'MINDFULNESS & THE JOURNEY OF BEREAVEMENT'
PETER BRIDGEWATER

CHAPTER THREE

FLOURISHING AT WORK

FINDING FULFILMENT AT WORK
DOESN'T ALWAYS REQUIRE A DRASTIC
CHANGE; SOMETIMES ADDRESSING
CONFLICTS AND RELATIONSHIPS
IN THE WORKPLACE CAN MAKE
ALL THE DIFFERENCE.

TURNING WORK
INTO PRODUCTIVE PLAY

◆

'It's impossible', said Pride.

'It's risky', said Experience.

'It's pointless', said Reason.

'Give it a try,' whispered The Heart.

ANON

42

HAPPINESS AT WORK

If you want more happiness at work, if you want to develop self-confidence and healthy relationships, you first have to learn that competition, rivalry, expectations and rules do not generate happiness, self-confidence or healthy relationships. In fact, they perpetuate discontentment.

FROM 'MINDFULNESS AT WORK'
MARIA ARPA

SUSTAINABILITY

Money is not a need;

it is a strategy for meeting needs.

FROM 'MINDFULNESS AT WORK'
MARIA ARPA

The Mindful Approach

◆

Sometimes we think we are dealing with the problem in front of us, when in actual fact we are trying to resolve an issue that persists in our life. This means our reactions may seem disproportionate to the person in front of us, which then escalates the issue.

FROM 'MINDFULNESS AT WORK'
MARIA ARPA

The Honest Audit

*Achieving balance is not a
moment-by-moment process. It is a flow
based on a foundation of wellbeing and
self-care. If we accept that it is impossible
to continuously balance it all, we can
liberate ourselves to enjoy the
uniqueness of each day.*

FROM 'MINDFULNESS AT WORK'
MARIA ARPA

BREATHE

Notice your breathing:

inhale, exhale, relax.

FROM 'MINDFULNESS AT WORK'
MARIA ARPA

BALANCE

*Achieving a work/life balance does
not mean equal time for both. It is a fluid
proposition that changes and fluctuates
according to the demands being made on you
and how you meet them. You achieve balance
when you have the integrated self-responsibility
to meet your obligations while also having the
confidence to set boundaries that keep
your life rewarding.*

FROM 'MINDFULNESS AT WORK'
MARIA ARPA

THE LESSON

*Education is about finding out who you are
and becoming your true self.*

FROM 'SOIL. SOUL. SOCIETY'
SATISH KUMAR

Now

*If you believe that feeling bad or worrying
long enough will change a past or future event,
then you are residing on another planet with
a different reality system.*

WILLIAM JAMES

WAKE UP & SMELL THE COFFEE

Do you want to find peace with yourself so you can continue on your current path or do you want to find the strength to make a change?

FROM 'MINDFULNESS AT WORK'
MARIA ARPA

LEARNING

Insanity is doing the same thing over
and over again and expecting different results.

ALBERT EINSTEIN

RESPONSIBILITY

Sometimes circumstances will reduce or change your options, but you always have the power to choose how you react and respond to whatever is in front of you.

FROM 'MINDFULNESS AT WORK'
MARIA ARPA

STAYING PRESENT

◆

*Before you can be of use to anyone in a
conflict, you need to be in a compassionate state.
This means to be aware of yourself, to have some
cognition and comprehension of your own
triggers and behaviours and to understand
what is going on inside you.*

FROM 'MINDFULNESS AT WORK'
MARIA ARPA

FREEDOM

*One of the most common traps we fall into
is feeling stuck and one of the most common ways
we make ourselves stuck is by struggling to keep
within our comfort zone instead of actively
moving to the edges in a structured and
informed way.*

FROM 'MINDFULNESS AT WORK'
MARIA ARPA

MAKING CHANGE

In an ideal world, your work would be a source of fulfilment, providing you with meaning and purpose. When the world around you isn't performing how you would like, your choices are either a change of attitude or a change of direction.

FROM 'MINDFULNESS AT WORK'
MARIA ARPA

RELEASING YOUR DEFENCES

Allow rather than control. Recognize what you are defending and imagine what it would be like to let go of defending.

FROM 'MINDFULNESS AT WORK'
MARIA ARPA

CHAPTER FOUR

FINDING
YOUR PATH

WALK ANY PATH AND OBSTACLES WILL
ARISE. IT IS THE NATURE OF THE WORLD
TO CONFRONT US WITH THE UNWANTED.
A MINDFUL APPROACH TO LIFE IS ABOUT
EMBRACING WHATEVER IMPEDES OUR
FLOW OR BLOCKS OUR WAY. RECONCILE
YOURSELF WITH THE UNGAINLY ASPECTS
OF REALITY AND FIND THE FREEDOM
TO MOVE BEYOND THEM.

KNOW

*Do not go upon what has
been acquired by repeated hearing,
by tradition, by rumour, by scripture, by
conjecture, by inference, or by product of mere
reasoning, or because it conforms with one's
preconceived notions, or because it is
authoritative, or because of the
status of your teacher…
Know for yourself.*

THE BUDDHA

PAIN

Pain is part of life. Only a living body can feel pain. Physical pain is obvious but we also have to endure psychological, emotional and spiritual pains. This is the first noble truth of existence.

FROM 'SOIL. SOUL. SOCIETY'
SATISH KUMAR

JUST STANDING

Pick a quiet place where you won't be disturbed. For the next five minutes give yourself completely to not having to go anywhere or do anything. Gaze softly, breathe naturally. Become aware of the body as a whole.

FROM 'MINDFULNESS FOR BLACK DOGS & BLUE DAYS'
RICHARD GILPIN

ESTABLISHING A PATH

*If our values give us our bearings and
our actions propel us forward, then mindfulness
is the manner in which we may travel.*

FROM 'MINDFULNESS FOR BLACK DOGS & BLUE DAYS'
RICHARD GILPIN

SOMETHING GOOD WILL COME

I have become my own version of an optimist. If I can't make it through one door, I'll go through another door — or I'll make a door. Something terrific will come no matter how dark the present.

FROM 'SOIL. SOUL. SOCIETY'
SATISH KUMAR

FINDING A FOOTHOLD

Knowing what matters, honouring our limits and paying attention to how we put in the time is what gives life much-needed momentum.

FROM 'MINDFULNESS FOR BLACK DOGS & BLUE DAYS'
RICHARD GILPIN

POTENTIAL

Regardless of how dark and downbeat the places you may find yourself, there always exists the potential of another path.

FROM 'MINDFULNESS FOR BLACK DOGS & BLUE DAYS'
RICHARD GILPIN

SELF-KNOWLEDGE

Know thyself.

INSCRIPTION AT THE TEMPLE OF APOLLO, DELPHI

FREEING SOME SPACE

Addressing the impact of critical life events is often simpler than we imagine. This frees up emotional space that allows us to move on in life.

FROM 'MINDFULNESS FOR BLACK DOGS & BLUE DAYS'
RICHARD GILPIN

GREAT DIVIDES

Cultivate a habit of healthy stopping. The interludes between acitivities are the punctuation points of our lives, offering opportunities for reflecting on and digesting experiences.

FROM 'MINDFULNESS FOR BLACK DOGS & BLUE DAYS'
RICHARD GILPIN

LIFE MATTERS

Life satisfaction is determined less by material acquisition and more by a sense of meaning, purpose, personal growth, healthy relationships and self-acceptance.

FROM 'MINDFULNESS FOR BLACK DOGS & BLUE DAYS'
RICHARD GILPIN

Fresh Prints on an Old Trail

◆

The present is your one chance to be fully

alive to your experience...

FROM 'MINDFULNESS FOR BLACK DOGS & BLUE DAYS'
RICHARD GILPIN

SUBLIME CONTRADICTIONS

*This is the essential paradox of
the mindful path: change occurs when we
are least striving for it.*

FROM 'MINDFULNESS FOR BLACK DOGS & BLUE DAYS'
RICHARD GILPIN

CHOOSING A MAP

Feelings are not reliable guides when we are in the grip of disorientating inner gloom.

FROM 'MINDFULNESS FOR BLACK DOGS & BLUE DAYS'
RICHARD GILPIN

SIGNPOSTS FOR THE WAY AHEAD

Embrace all parts of yourself with warm attention and interest; thus you will loosen emotional knots and give your faults space to transform themselves.

FROM 'MINDFULNESS FOR BLACK DOGS & BLUE DAYS'
RICHARD GILPIN

WISDOM

◆

Do not ignore the effect of right action,
saying, 'This will come to nothing'. A pitcher is
filled with water by a steady stream of drops;
likewise, the wise person improves and achieves
wellbeing a little at a time.

THE BUDDHA

DEFINING THE UNDEFINABLE

◆

The practice of mindfulness is merely the development of your innate capacity to be aware. Rather than trying to get somewhere, or achieve something, mindfulness is more about coming home.

FROM 'MINDFULNESS FOR BLACK DOGS & BLUE DAYS'
RICHARD GILPIN

OUTSIDE

◆

As little as five minutes of daily outdoor activity in any green space, but especially in wilderness areas or near water, will significantly boost mood, self-esteem and mental health.

FROM 'MINDFULNESS FOR BLACK DOGS & BLUE DAYS'
RICHARD GILPIN

CHAPTER FIVE

THE
NATURAL HEART

CARING FOR SOIL, FOR NATURE,
FOR THE ENVIRONMENT IS A MORAL
IMPERATIVE. HAVE COURAGE TO
LIVE SIMPLY BUT LIVE WELL
AND JOYFULLY.

HANDLING NOISE

Before we can carry our own inner silence out into the noisy world, we need to identify it, to know it as a friend. Everyone who has found this inner silence will have discovered it in their own different way. We can find it even when simply standing by a gatepost.

FROM 'SEEKING SILENCE IN A NOISY WORLD'
ADAM FORD

EXTREME SILENCE

*Find a field or a forest where the world and
its noise are out of sight and far away, where
the sun and the sky, the earth and the water all
speak the same language, reminding you that
you are here to develop like the things
that grow all around you.*

FROM 'SEEKING SILENCE IN A NOISY WORLD'
ADAM FORD

BEING & DOING

*Being fully absorbed in the moment
while attending to an action requires
concentration and practice. Doing something
mindfully involves being fully present in the act
itself, and being conscious of not performing a
task while thinking of something else.*

FROM 'THE ART OF MINDFUL GARDENING'
ARK REDWOOD

WINTER

———————◆———————

Winter is the time to be still, and to reflect;

it is the yin of the year.

FROM 'THE ART OF MINDFUL GARDENING'
ARK REDWOOD

PERCEPTION

A bee perceives yellow flowers as rich shades of purple. We say a daffodil is yellow, but this is only relatively true. It is not an absolute truth.

FROM 'THE ART OF MINDFUL GARDENING'
ARK REDWOOD

MINDFUL FOCUS

'Instruct' the mind to stay focused, and not shoot off in all directions. Whenever attention wanders, bring it calmly back to the breath.

FROM 'THE ART OF MINDFUL GARDENING'
ARK REDWOOD

The Perfect Plant

It is beholden on the wise gardener to provide the optimum conditions possible for the seed to grow into the perfect plant.

FROM 'The Art of Mindful Gardening'
ARK REDWOOD

SPRING

The compost you create for your garden will be used in the life cycle of another being. Today's flowers are tomorrow's cabbages.

FROM 'THE ART OF MINDFUL GARDENING'
ARK REDWOOD

THE LONG WALK

A good long walk takes us beyond the horizon — several times. We experience liberation, unique to walking, as countryside or town flow past us at an even human pace.

FROM 'THE ART OF MINDFUL WALKING'
ADAM FORD

ALLOWING & RELEASING

*Sometimes we carry a burden from the day;
a hurt, an anger or an unhappy recollection.
The end of the day is the time to let these
things go. Note these thoughts, face
them and acknowledge them —
and then dismiss them.*

FROM 'THE ART OF MINDFUL WALKING'
ADAM FORD

THE DAILY WALK

It can be easier to break a habit than
it is to establish one. We may sometimes feel
lazy and reluctant to bother with a daily walk,
especially if the weather is uninviting, wet, windy
or cold; but it always turns out to be
worth the effort.

FROM 'THE ART OF MINDFUL WALKING'
ADAM FORD

CENTRING MEDITATION

The purpose of meditation is not to get rid of all the discomfort, but simply to notice what it is. Do that by breathing and returning again and again to yourself. Be curious and compassionate with yourself.

FROM 'ZEN & THE ART OF RAISING CHICKENS'
CLEA DANAAN

NATURAL HAPPINESS

◆

The happiness we find in the natural world is irreplaceable and it is something we can all connect with. It is in all of us. Our innate affiliation with the natural world means that when we spend time in nature's company, we can open up to letting contentment, ease, peace and vitality into our lives. Nature captures our sensory experience, our curiosity and our attention and naturally brings us out of our thinking minds and back to the present moment.

FROM 'MINDFULNESS & THE NATURAL WORLD'
CLAIRE THOMPSON

RIDING THE WAVE

*Imagine swimming in an ocean. The waves
are your thoughts and emotions and they will
take you where they please. Now imagine you are
on a surfboard, riding the waves and enjoying the
tide as the waves come and go. You can even watch
the waves go by. Mindfulness is your surfboard.
Your thoughts and emotions are all transitory.
If we notice this, they no longer need to
dictate our behaviour.*

FROM 'MINDFULNESS & THE NATURAL WORLD'
CLAIRE THOMPSON

ALL IS CONNECTED

The universe created us, yet we act as though we are separate from it. This sense of detachment is a delusion that imprisons our hearts and minds.

FROM 'EINSTEIN & THE ART OF MINDFUL CYCLING'
BEN IRVINE

Go Wild

*Go out in the wild…and open your
heart and mind to the mystery, magic and
majesty of the natural world.*

FROM 'SOIL. SOUL. SOCIETY'
SATISH KUMAR

LEAVING SPACE

◆

Leave a little space for appreciation and contemplation of the simple things around you; the opportunity to marvel at the natural world is everywhere, at every moment. It is in us and around us and it provides us with most of the things we have in our lives.

FROM 'MINDFULNESS & THE NATURAL WORLD'
CLAIRE THOMPSON

FINDING JOY

Just as it's hard to be solemn on a pogo stick, meditative on a rodeo horse or presidential on a Segway, it's almost impossible to be in a bad mood on a bike.

FROM 'EINSTEIN & THE ART OF MINDFUL CYCLING'
BEN IRVINE

CHAPTER SIX

Paying Attention, Finding Balance

TAKE CARE OF THE SOUL AND
CULTIVATE LOVE, COMPASSION,
BEAUTY AND UNITY TO REALIZE
HARMONY WITHIN AND
HARMONY WITHOUT.

Awareness...

*Our thoughts often take us away from
the direct experience of our lives in the
present moment. We often get lost and involved
in them. But we don't need to. Notice your
thoughts in your everyday life. Notice what
they are telling you and whether it is true or
helpful. You may be surprised to see how many
thoughts you have and find it difficult to
separate them out. That's OK.*

FROM 'MINDFULNESS & THE NATURAL WORLD'
CLAIRE THOMPSON

...AND ALLOWING

Being mindful of your thoughts will get easier with practice. When you notice your thoughts, don't hold on to them or push them away. They all come and go and are constantly changing. Just let them be as they are.

FROM 'MINDFULNESS & THE NATURAL WORLD'
CLAIRE THOMPSON

FLOW

*Pleasurable and painful thoughts
and emotions will come and go all the time.
We can't hold onto them, push them away or
make them stay with us forever. All we can do
is accept them. And remember that we can
be comforted by the fact they will
always be changing.*

FROM 'MINDFULNESS & THE NATURAL WORLD'
CLAIRE THOMPSON

FIND CONTENTMENT

The Buddha taught that our chief troubles come from not being content with what we have.

FROM 'MEDITATION & THE ART OF BEEKEEPING'
MARK MAGILL

INTENTION, PREPARATION, EFFORT

◆

*There is a Tibetan saying: 'If you
want to know your past, look at your present
conditions. If you want to know your future, look
at your present actions.' Intention, preparation,
effort. These are the factors that govern the results
of our actions. Whether they are done poorly or
with determination — with a positive or negative
attitude — affects how we will fare. It's far better
not to wait until the snow flies to realize
that winter is coming.*

FROM 'MEDITATION & THE ART OF BEEKEEPING'
MARK MAGILL

THIS MOMENT

At this moment, allow everything to be as it is.

FROM 'MINDFULNESS & THE ART OF MANAGING ANGER'
MIKE FISHER

ADAPTING

Finding balance means accommodating change. That is the basis of adaptation.

FROM 'MEDITATION & THE ART OF BEEKEEPING'
MARK MAGILL

APPROACHING STILLNESS

*If we allow ourselves to be constantly
lost in our thinking minds, we will be forever
in conflict, always ill at ease.*

FROM 'HAPPINESS & HOW IT HAPPENS'
THE HAPPY BUDDHA

FINDING PERSPECTIVE

When you look back over your life,
what sort of person do you want to see?

FROM 'EINSTEIN & THE ART OF MINDFUL CYCLING'
BEN IRVINE

ESTABLISHING MINDFULNESS

*Developing mindfulness is like developing
any skill, such as playing a musical instrument,
performing surgery or flying a lunar module —
the idea is to build and consolidate our
capabilities in a controlled environment
before applying our learning to
real-life situations.*

FROM 'EINSTEIN & THE ART OF MINDFUL CYCLING'
BEN IRVINE

ZEN

Zen is about noticing, and it's a practice
you have to do yourself. No one can notice things
for you. You can read and talk and read some
more but until you practice it, either on a
meditation cushion or through daily life
(or even better, both), you will not discover
the truths and freedom on the other side.

FROM 'ZEN & THE ART OF MINDFUL PARENTING'
CLEA DANAAN

NOTICING

Mindfulness is about tapping into the human capacity to notice, and to tease apart the conditioning we carry about the ego / mind and presence.

FROM 'ZEN & THE ART OF MINDFUL PARENTING'
CLEA DANAAN

CHAPTER SEVEN

TOGETHERNESS

LIVING CONSCIOUSLY LEADS
TO SELF-RESPONSIBILITY, WHICH IN
A RELATIONSHIP LEADS TO POWER-
SHARING, EQUALITY AND TRUST.

BEING VULNERABLE

Showing emotional vulnerability may make us fear rejection. But once you become accustomed to doing it, it will become a way of life and will build self-confidence.

FROM 'THE HEART OF MINDFUL RELATIONSHIPS'
MARIA ARPA

STILLING JUDGEMENT

*If you find yourself judging and
blaming others for how you feel, stop.*

FROM 'THE HEART OF MINDFUL RELATIONSHIPS'
MARIA ARPA

MAKING CHANGE

◆

There is a very big difference between compromising on needs and changing the way we meet our needs. Many people are not content with their lives, but are frightened of the steps they would need to take to bring about the real change they seek.

FROM 'THE HEART OF MINDFUL RELATIONSHIPS'
MARIA ARPA

THE CREATIVE PATH TO AWARENESS

◆

*When practised mindfully, drawing
has the power to effortlessly lead us into a
deeper relationship with ourselves and the world
around us; turning drawing into play, into a
dance of movement, an act of seeing deeply
and connecting profoundly with life.*

FROM 'MINDFULNESS & THE ART OF DRAWING'
WENDY ANN GREENHALGH

117

BECOMING

Your beliefs become your thoughts, your thoughts become your words, your words become your actions, your actions become your habits, your habits become your values, your values become your destiny.

MAHATMA GANDHI

FLOURISHING

---◆---

What is more important in order for humans to flourish: conformity or connection?

FROM 'THE HEART OF MINDFUL RELATIONSHIPS'
MARIA ARPA

Connections

None of us can exist in isolation.
Our lives and existence are supported by others
in seen and unseen ways, be it parents, mentors or
society at large. To be aware of these connections,
to feel appreciation for them and to strive to give
something back to society in a spirit of gratitude
is the proper way for human beings to live.

DAISAKU IKEDA

DRAWING CLOSER

*When we're drawing, we are spending
time with something, a place, an object, scene
or person, and in doing so; we draw closer, and
come into relationship with it. In truth, drawing
is all about relationship, because it requires us to
build connections with the world around us, to
get to know it better and deeper, through the
process happening on the page.*

FROM 'MINDFULNESS & THE ART OF DRAWING'
WENDY ANN GREENHALGH

CHAPTER EIGHT

The Heart
of the Home

WHEN YOU ADD ARTIFICIAL
INGREDIENTS, YOU MAY BE TAKEN
ON A JOURNEY OF CRAVING THAT
IS DIFFICULT TO SATISFY. WHEN YOU
BAKE YOUR OWN BREAD YOU ARE THE
CREATOR OF SIMPLE FOOD THAT
WILL MEET YOUR BODY'S NEEDS
AND GIVE YOU CONFIDENCE
IN WHAT YOU EAT.

SYNERGY

An agreeable combination of chords in music can evoke a real sense of harmony — a bit like bread-and-butter. When baking, our hands act like conductors, mixing up ingredients to achieve harmony of texture and flavour. The key elements in achieving this are, first, respect for the integrity that rests in wholeness; and, second, appreciating the potential for a harmonious synergy that comes when diverse elements are combined.

FROM 'THE ART OF MINDFUL BAKING'
JULIA PONSONBY

CREATIVE TOGETHERNESS

*Cooking together becomes a bit like
'jamming', to use a musical term. It's an
opportunity to be creative together, to share ideas.
This element of play is something that we can all
bring to our baking; it is an often-forgotten
aspect of the meditative approach that
brings revitalization and joy.*

FROM 'THE ART OF MINDFUL BAKING'
JULIA PONSONBY

SIMPLICITY

Like breathing, simplicity has a fundamental presence that spreads harmony into art, health, culture — perhaps into all things, because it too is one of life's great universals. Can we therefore use simplicity as a kind of 'litmus test' for what is good and wholesome about food?

FROM 'THE ART OF MINDFUL BAKING'
JULIA PONSONBY

By Hand

Our hands are our most immediate tools,
and they work in perfect harmony with our
brains and our emotions to manifest the diverse
possibilities that grow in our imaginations…
Whether it is in the construction of an awe-inspiring
temple or a tiny hut, a dramatic sculpture or a
simple pot, a lavish dinner or a humble loaf,
our hands are there making the moves.

FROM 'THE ART OF MINDFUL BAKING'
JULIA PONSONBY

LOVE & LIGHT

◆

*One way to bring consciousness
and love into your cooking is to chant,
either aloud or to yourself. Use a tried-and-tested
mantra that you know works for you, or create a
new one. Try 'Love and light with each bite' or
'Bring health and heal with every meal'.
The intention is to focus love into your
food and to prevent negativity from
entering your cooking.*

FROM 'THE ART OF MINDFUL BAKING'
JULIA PONSONBY

TUNING IN

A mantra can be useful when you feel particularly vulnerable to negative emotions. Baking is your opportunity to tune into the goodness of the task at hand, and mantras can assist this tuning.

FROM 'THE ART OF MINDFUL BAKING'
JULIA PONSONBY

SOME FLOUR MUST FALL...

*Like gardeners, cooks need to be prepared
to get messy, in order to get to grips with some of
their ingredients. Baking gives us the opportunity
to confront these undulations of orderliness
without 'flipping out', and to experience them
as simply a mini-cycle within a broader
cycle of ongoing life.*

FROM 'THE ART OF MINDFUL BAKING'
JULIA PONSONBY

130

BECOME THE BREAD

◆

Baking also allows you to be creative
and to identify yourself with an alternative
reality — you put a bit of yourself into your
baking and, on one level, you become your
easy-rising bread, cake or scone.

FROM 'THE ART OF MINDFUL BAKING'
JULIA PONSONBY

BEGINNING FRESH

◆

When we engage as beginners — our minds are fresh, open to the possibilities of that moment. It is this 'beginner's mind' that many adults set out to cultivate when they consciously introduce a mindful approach to their lives.

FROM 'THE ART OF MINDFUL BAKING'
JULIA PONSONBY

Ripening

*If we wish to gain ripeness and sweetness
we must go through the heat of self-discipline.
Even grains and vegetables ripened by the sun
need to go through the heat of the stove in order
to become edible and digestible. Unless we
practise self-discipline, we cannot transform
ourselves from being to becoming.*

FROM 'SOIL. SOUL. SOCIETY'
SATISH KUMAR

CHAPTER NINE

CLEARING
THE RED MIST

LEARN TO USE YOUR ANGER IN A
CONSTRUCTIVE AND HEALTHY WAY;
MINDFULNESS WILL BE YOUR
GUIDING LIGHT.

LETTING GO

Resentment is like drinking poison and waiting for it to kill your enemy.

FROM 'THE HEART OF MINDFUL RELATIONSHIPS'
MARIA ARPA

THE PATH

◆

ZEN BUDDHISM'S FOUR NOBLE TRUTHS:

1. *Life is suffering.*

2. *Suffering has an origin.*

3. *Suffering can cease.*

4. *There is a path out of suffering.*

FROM 'ZEN & THE ART OF MINDFUL PARENTING'
CLEA DANAAN

TRUE ZEN

There is a misconception that Zen or meditation in general is about being unflappable, or calm in every moment. But the point is simply to become aware of what is happening. This is easy when what is happening is a lovely butterfly settling airily on a flower. But this exercises nothing, except an appreciation of beauty. No small thing — but not something that pushes us.

FROM 'ZEN & THE ART OF MINDFUL PARENTING'
CLEA DANAAN

BEING PUSHED

◆

*It is in being pushed, noticing that
we are being pushed, and then being present
that we find our way.*

FROM 'ZEN & THE ART OF MINDFUL PARENTING'
CLEA DANAAN

LETTING GO OF ATTACHMENT

◆

What we own is not who we are.

FROM 'MINDFULNESS & THE ART OF MANAGING ANGER'
MIKE FISHER

EMBRACING THE POLARITIES

◆

Every time a person triggers your anger,
in that very moment they become your guru or
teacher. They are offering you the opportunity to
embrace the polarities in yourself and to view the
world from an entirely different perspective.

FROM 'MINDFULNESS & THE ART OF MANAGING ANGER'
MIKE FISHER

You

You yourself, as much as anybody in the entire universe, deserve your love and affection.

THE BUDDHA

OPENING TO STILLNESS

Train yourself to relax by exploring different ways to slow down and become still. Focusing on just one activity will bring you right into the present.

FROM 'MINDFULNESS & THE ART OF MANAGING ANGER'
MIKE FISHER

OPENING YOUR HEART

You can close your eyes to the things you do not want to see, but you cannot close your heart to the things you do not want to feel.

FROM 'MINDFULNESS & THE ART OF MANAGING ANGER'
MIKE FISHER

MANAGING ANGER

In order to control your anger,

you must express it.

FROM 'MINDFULNESS & THE ART OF MANAGING ANGER'
MIKE FISHER

SURVIVING ANGER

◆

*Survivors of other people's anger develop
an acute sense of anticipating the behaviour of
others in a constant effort to avoid conflict. They
contain their thoughts and feelings to
keep out of danger's way.*

FROM 'MINDFULNESS & THE ART OF MANAGING ANGER'
MIKE FISHER

Becoming Your Own Teacher

No one saves us but ourselves. No one can and no one may. We ourselves must walk the path.

THE BUDDHA

How Are You?

◆

It is all too easy to lose focus on what is
happening in our internal world, on how we are
feeling physically and emotionally. Next time
someone asks 'How are you?', take the
opportunity to tune in to yourself, take
a moment to reflect — and then give
an honest answer.

FROM 'MINDFULNESS & THE ART OF MANAGING ANGER'
MIKE FISHER

BEFRIENDING STILLNESS

*Take time out from 'doing' to allow space
for the soul to deepen and breathe. Befriending
stillness and solitude will lead you
to tranquility.*

FROM MINDFULNESS & THE ART OF MANAGING ANGER'
MIKE FISHER

BLESSING

WHEREVER YOUR PATH NEXT TAKES YOU, MAY IT BE A STEP TOWARDS WHATEVER IS RICH AND MEANINGFUL FOR YOU. MAY YOU FIND LASTING CONTENTMENT AND EASE, AND MAY YOU ENCOUNTER THE SUBLIME SILENCES, NAMELESS JOYS AND GREAT MYSTERIES OF BEING THAT LIE BEYOND WORDS.

NOTES

NOTES

NOTES

THE MINDFULNESS SERIES

◆

The Art of Mindful Baking
Julia Ponsonby
ISBN: 978-1-78240-080-6

The Art of Mindful Birdwatching
Clare Thompson
ISBN: 978-1-78240-428-6

The Art of Mindful Gardening
Ark Redwood
ISBN: 978-1-907332-59-3

The Art of Mindful Silence
Adam Ford
ISBN: 978-1-908005-11-3

The Art of Mindful Singing
Jeremy Dion
ISBN: 978-1-78240-419-4

The Art of Mindful Walking
Adam Ford
ISBN: 978-1-907332-58-6

Einstein & the Art of Mindful Cycling
Ben Irvine
ISBN: 978-1-908005-47-2

Galileo & the Art of Ageing Mindfully
Adam Ford
ISBN: 978-1-78240-243-5

Happiness & How it Happens
The Happy Buddha
ISBN: 978-1-907332-93-7

The Heart of Mindful Relationships
Maria Arpa
ISBN: 978-1-908005-29-8

The Joy of Mindful Writing
Joy Kenward
ISBN: 978-1-78240-504-7

The Mindful Art of Wild Swimming
Tessa Wardley
ISBN: 978-1-78240-429-3

The Mindful Man
Caspar Walsh
ISBN: 978-1-78240-566-5

Mindful Pregnancy & Birth
Riga Forbes
ISBN: 978-1-78240-505-4

Mindfulness & Compassion
The Happy Buddha
ISBN: 978-1-78240-288-6

Mindfulness & Music
Mark Tanner
ISBN: 978-1-78240-567-2

Mindfulness & Surfing
Sam Bleakley
ISBN: 978-1-78240-329-6

*Mindfulness & the
Art of Drawing*
Wendy Ann Greenhalgh
ISBN: 978-1-78240-283-1

*Mindfulness & the Art of
Managing Anger*
Mike Fisher
ISBN: 978-1-908005-30-4

*Mindfulness & the
Art of Urban Living*
Adam Ford
ISBN: 978-1-908005-77-9

*Mindfulness & the
Journey of Bereavement*
Peter Bridgewater
ISBN: 978-1-78240-206-0

*Mindfulness &
the Natural World*
Claire Thompson
ISBN: 978-1-78240-102-5

Mindfulness at Work
Maria Arpa
ISBN: 978-1-908005-76-2

*Mindfulness for
Black Dogs & Blue Days*
Richard Gilpin
ISBN: 978-1-907332-92-0

*Mindfulness for
Unravelling Anxiety*
Richard Gilpin
ISBN: 978-1-78240-318-0

The Mindfulness in Knitting
Rachael Matthews
ISBN: 978-1-78240-418-7

Naturally Mindful
ISBN: 978-1-78240-416-3

*Zen & the Path of
Mindful Parenting*
Clea Danaan
ISBN: 978-1-78240-154-4

INDEX

◆

ACKNOWLEDGEMENTS

◆

The publisher would like to thank Maria Arpa,
Peter Bridgewater, Clea Danaan, Mike Fisher, Adam Ford,
Richard Gilpin, Wendy Ann Greenhalgh, The Happy Buddha, Ben Irvine,
Satish Kumar, Mark Magill, Julia Ponsonby, Ark Redwood
& Claire Thompson.